Jesus and You
Jesus y tu

"I am so proud of the work that Jeanette and Moisés have put in to making this book what it is! They are two of the best people I know and to see their combined passions culminate in this book is amazing. As far as the book is concerned, I can think of no better way to train up a child than to start with reading the creation account and such encouraging words over them. Can't wait to get mine for my kids' bedtime!"

Pastor Alex Murphy, Greenville, Ohio

Jesus and You
Jesus y tu

God Created All Things
Dios creo todas las cosas

Jeanette Walker

Illustrated and Translated
by Moisés Medina

*Ilustrado y traducido
por Moisés Medina*

BROOKSTONE
PUBLISHING GROUP

Birmingham, Alabama

Jesus and You

Brookstone Publishing Group
An imprint of Iron Stream Media
100 Missionary Ridge
Birmingham, AL 35242
IronStreamMedia.com

Library of Congress Cataloging-in-Publication Data
Names: Walker, Jeanette, 1962- author. | Medina Estevez, Moises, illustrator, translator. | Walker, Jeanette, 1962- Jesus and you. English. | Walker, Jeanette, 1962- Jesus and you. Spanish.
Title: Jesus and you : God created all things = Jesus y tu : Dios creo todas las cosas / Jeanette Walker ; illustrated and translated by Moises Medina Estevez.
Other titles: Jesus y tu : Dios creo todas las cosas
Description: Birmingham, Alabama : Brookstone Publishing Group, [2025] | Audience: Ages 3-5 | English and Spanish. | Summary: "Jesus and You! gently guides little eyes to grasp the wonder of God's creation, helping parents teach their children the powerful truth that God is the Creator of all. This story encourages both children and adults to pause and marvel at the beauty of the world-and to remember that God's hand is behind every part of it"-- Provided by publisher.
Identifiers: LCCN 2024058911 | ISBN 9781960814128 (paperback) | ISBN 9781960814135 (epub)
Subjects: LCSH: Creation--Juvenile literature. | Bible. Genesis, I-II, 2--Juvenile literature.
Classification: LCC BS651 .W247 2025 | DDC 222/.11--dc23/eng/20250416
LC record available at https://lccn.loc.gov/2024058911

Cover design by For the Muse Designs

ISBN: 978-1-960814-12-8 (paperback)
ISBN: 978-1-960814-13-5 (ebook)

1 2 3 4 5—29 28 27 26 25

Thank you, Jesus, for giving me this book. I dedicate this book to my grandsons, Griffin and Asher. I pray that along with them each child would come to know Jesus as their Lord and Savior and to serve Him all the days of their lives. Thank you, Moises, for the beautiful drawings that bring His story to life. —JW

Gracias. Thank God for the opportunity to express His love with the talents that he entrusted to me. And thanks to Nettie for inviting me to be part of this beautiful book. —MM

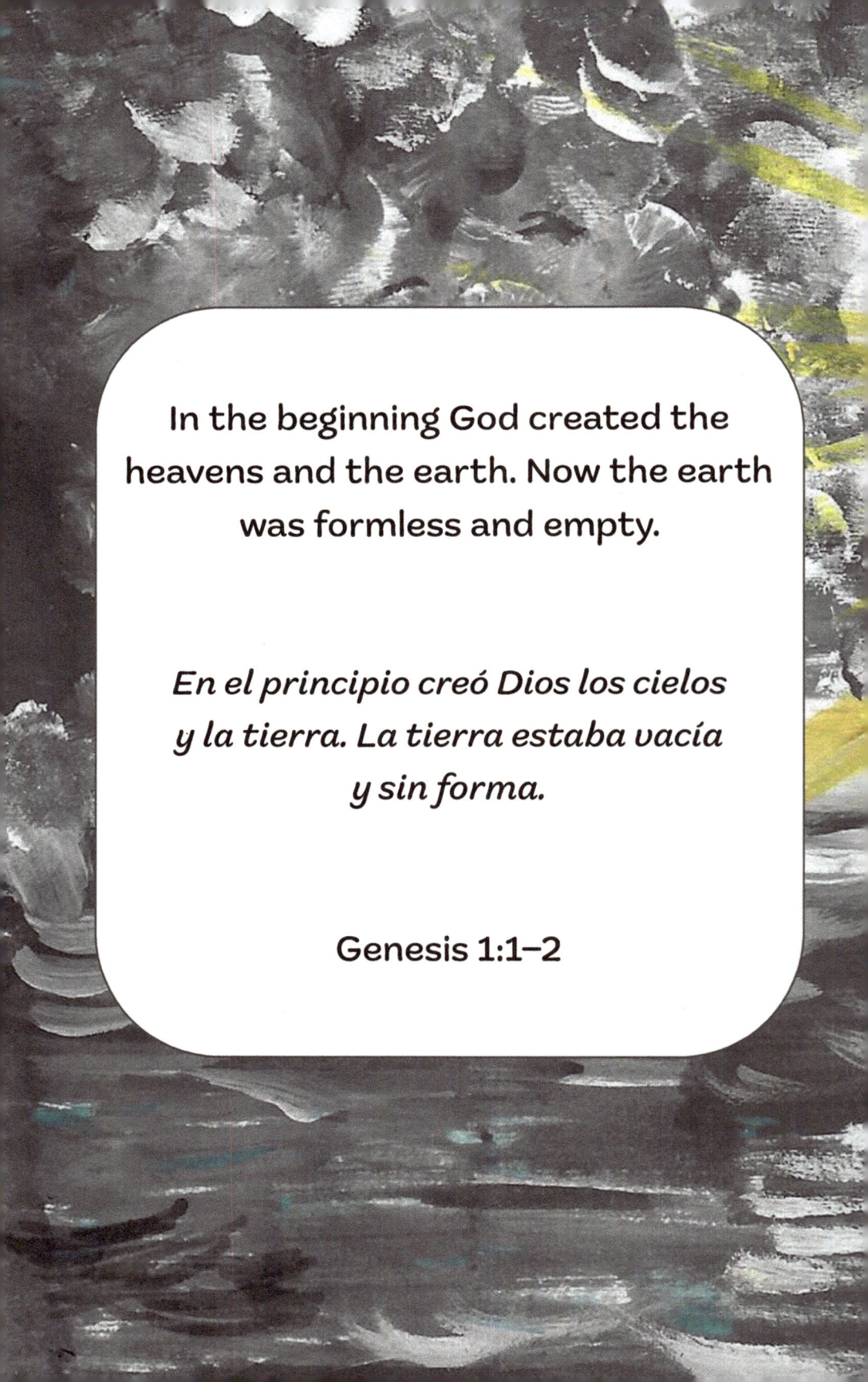

In the beginning God created the heavens and the earth. Now the earth was formless and empty.

En el principio creó Dios los cielos y la tierra. La tierra estaba vacía y sin forma.

Genesis 1:1–2

God called the light "day."

Dios llamó a la luz «día».

Genesis 1:5

god made the day

Dios hizo el dia.

Jesus loves you more than all the stars
in the sky!

*¡Jesús te ama más que todas las estrellas
del cielo!*

Then God said, "Let the earth produce vegetation."

Entonces Dios dijo: «Que la tierra produzca vegetación.»

Genesis 1:11

Then God said, "Let the waters swarm with fish and other life."

Entonces Dios dijo: «Que las aguas se llenen de peces y otros vivos.»

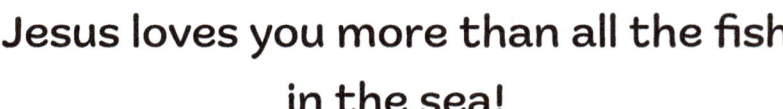

Genesis 1:20

Jesus loves you more than all the fish in the sea!

¡Jesús te ama más que a todos los peces del mar!

God made the waters and all the sea creatures too!!

Dios hizo las aguas y todas las criaturas que allí viven.

Then God said, "Let the earth produce living creatures."

Entonces Dios dijo: «Que la tierra produzca criaturas vivientes.»

Genesis 1:24

pig
cochino

Lion
Leόn

Cow
Yaca

Sheep
oveja

Then God said, "Let us make man."

Entonces Dios dijo: «Hagamos al hombre.»

Genesis 1:26

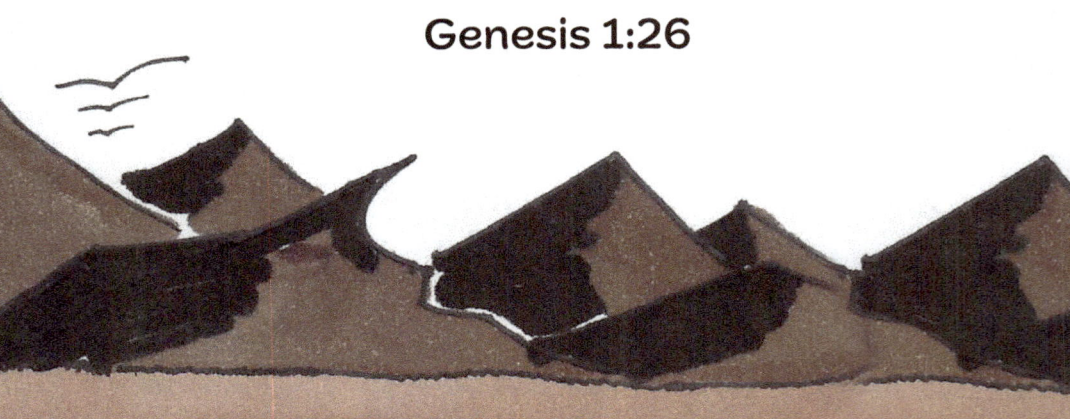

Then the Lord God formed a woman from the rib that he had taken from the man.

Entonces el Señor Dios formó una mujer de la costilla que le había quitado al hombre.

Genesis 2:22

this is the first woman.
Esta es la primer mujer.

God named her Eve.
Dios la llamo: Eva.

I knew you before you were born.

Te conocí antes de que nacieras.

Jeremiah 1:5

And best of all, God made you!

¡Y lo mejor de todo es que Dios te hizo!

And the Lord God took the man and put
him in the garden to keep it.

*Y el Señor Dios tomó al hombre y lo puso
en el jardín para que lo guardara.*

Genesis 2:15

On the seventh day God
had completed his work that he
had done, and he rested.

En el séptimo día, Dios terminó la obra
que había hecho, y descansó.

Genesis 2:2